The True Masterminds of Manipulation

Authored by Bobby R. Simonds

I0423466

I dedicate this to all of whom, may question the world today; Religions, the Governments, the Media, and mainly, the *Manipulators*; UFO's, Aliens, etc.

As they say, *"There is a sucker for everything..."*

I do not believe this to be true, and neither should you...

Prologue

I cannot even begin to express to you, how easily folks manipulated into believing something to be true; or manipulated into purchasing something they did not need, let alone, want...or even have more than one, of the same exact item.

Many people forget, the possibility that they even own these *various* items, in which they end up purchasing again, because the commercial they may have heard or seen, sounded so convincing.

Here is an example, from year to year; everything seems to be on a *repeated cycle*. Such as, theme related items. They change the product just slightly - forcing your brain to assume it is a new & improved item. Consequently, you became a victim into thinking you have to replace it! Moreover, this happens so often, that it is pretty much the copycat...of the original item.

We live in an *Age* of not knowing how to use methods, such as *Self-Control!*

For another example, you walk into any variety of *Superstores*, and as soon as you walk in, all of these bombard you, so-called discounted items.

Originally, you had a small list of various items you planned to purchase, and then you proceed to *cash-out*.

Meanwhile, while you are waiting for the person in front of you to hurry up, you start zooming in on the candy, gum, gift cards, or even those gossip magazines!

I am a 35-year-old man, and to my knowledge of various militia facts - made into fiction - I had to create this book, to share to the world of how bad, the manipulation has become in our world today.

Between the Fairy Tales of Religion and the constant lies from our governments - here in American, and throughout the globe - I thought I should take it upon myself to help provide a little enlightenment for you.

My goal from writing this book is not only to help you think for yourself, but perhaps, to help you get more of an understanding from a different perspective. In addition, pointing out certain aspects of our daily lives, which are obviously getting a bit out of control!

There are many various *Books* floating around in the market, with topics similar to mine. However, I am merely writing about my first-hand experiences, and I had included various theories behind the lies - that we are so used to hearing - and many people are tricked into believing to be true. *They* say, "The more people hear something, the more the human brain starts to think it to be true." If that is true, we are all in serious trouble!

Manipulation is a big part of life. Whether it is Religion, Politics, Family, the School System, various School Shootings, Oil Companies, the Media, Reality Shows, etc., it is all around us. Moreover, we need to start thinking for ourselves. I hope that, with my help, this will make it easier for you to defend yourself against the daily manipulation games.

Section 1:

The Hand of Manipulation

Chapter 1 - Religion

As far as global manipulation is concerned, I tend to recognize the biggest lie globally, is that of Religion. Moreover, for those who think that there is a difference between Religion & Organized Religion, well...you may want to rethink what you believe, to be known to you.

I recently had a short conversation with a "Jehovah Witness Volunteer". I told him that I do not believe in God, per say, but I am a Spiritual Believer. I also told him, that I believe that we are all connected thru the Universe, and that is as far as my beliefs go.

Ironically, he answered, "I totally understand where you're coming from. Religion is a business, and like any business, *they* manipulate the audience with the around-a-bout lie...that portrays truth. However, by no means, do *they* actually answer any questions within the Sermon at any various church. I swear, if *they* released the truth, there would be *Hell* to pay!"

I was a bit stunned that he was this truthful, and so honest with me. We have been talking on & off, for over two years. This was the first time; he would ever reveal my theories truthful, with the regards to Religion. In addition, he mentioned, when you are off at college - learning how to be a Minister - they do not teach you what the Bible means, or even answer any related questions to Religion. If anything, they are simply providing you how to sell Religion. In my opinion, this should be the first sign of questioning your religious beliefs.

Not long after our conversation, my wife, & I had, two women knock on our door. I had my wife answer the door, as to the fact I was writing this book.

As she opened the door, she had noticed that one of them was holding a Bible in their hand.

"Hello," the older woman said, "we wanted to explore the Bible." My wife, of course said, "No thanks, not interested", and shut the door.

My wife and I laughed as to the fact was, there was no *pitching* of the sales, but just getting straight to the point. I said to my wife, "What's to explore? More myths?"

I waited for the women to get into their car, and drive away.

We both had then walked outside, and my neighbor's response was, "Damn, Bible thumpers! They're persistent on selling Religion, aren't they?" I responded, "Isn't that what Sunday Church is for?"

If you question your beliefs with Religion, then you too, have a brain;

that thinks outside of the confinements of a box...without being conned. Religion is one of the most ancient lies, and/or cover-ups in humankind history. It's literally a global manipulation, and it not only disgusts me, but it saddens me to know, just how many people are believers of something they can't see, prove, or even, over-all understand, from a so-called Bible.

Sure, there are many facts inside this *Handbook* of Religion. However, when Religion was created, I believe it was for *straying man,* from knowing how the world & the universe truly works. People were more dense and single-minded back then, than we are now...I think...

In fact, almost every religion that
is to date has their own versions of *God*
or even *Jesus Christ*. In which of
course, I find to be quite ironic. To
my knowledge, Christianity & even
Catholicism are the oldest domination's
of religion.

I believe that it was easier for
them to create something so hopeful, to
help man, to have an easier way, to face
their own demise.

Nevertheless, when you have
Jehovah's Witness knocking on your front
door every week, you start to wonder the
sham it has become. Everyone is aware
of where each religious church is
located. There is not anything to sell

door to door. In my opinion, there are too many followers of Religion, and people need to start waking up.

You need to break free from Man's worst lie, and learn the spirituality of life, instead of being brainwashed by something that was obvious to some, that it was all made up!

I am assuming - aside from personal journals - with ancient humans, dating back to A.D., there were probably only a handful of people that knew how to write. Therefore, the scriptures were most likely, facts within fiction.

Ironically, how is it different with various stories in books today, now is it? I myself have often put facts into my fictional stories. The reason behind this objectivity is so you can then keep the readers interested in past, present, and/or even future context.

With that being said, why is the *Bible* any different? I cannot express enough to you, how many people tend to believe this mythical story about *Jesus Christ,* rising to life from his grave, just after being tortured and killed on a wooden cross, just some days before hand...

Okay, a wooden cross let us start with that - sounds simple, right. With your body standing, with your arms stretched out, then nailed against a wooden post...um, yah, it turns out to be the same design as a cross. However, it has nothing to do with a Religious Standpoint!

Second, when referring to *God* - even back then - it could have been an Alien or some giant man, which was more intellectual than the average person and that, is how that part was created.

Moreover, I am sorry for saying this, but in modern times, if a human were to rise from a grave; we call them Vampires or Zombies...not ***JESUS CHRIST!***

On the other hand, perhaps, they were not even fully dead to begin with. Back then, they did not have our modern medicine, so who has to say, they checked for the pulse correctly.

Perhaps, J.C., was just in a coma?

Perhaps, even he was in this coma, and

had an incredibly weak pulse...

When anyone researches Greek God's,

in modern times, it is generally

categorized with Greek Mythology. With

that being said, should not all

religions be considered Mythology?

Even various network channels, such

as, Discover or History channel

(networks) refers to Greek creatures or

God's (when it is associated with Greek

Religion), are always referenced as

mythical.

Therefore, why are people confused

with Catholicism, Christianity, Judaism,

and Islam's, Muslims, and many more titles of domination's, not considered Mythical?

Another thing that has continuously bothering me about Organized Religion is that they are very judgmental, and greedy. They have it written in their *Bible's* to donate 10% of your earnings to these various organizations... In addition, they charge a hefty fee for these religious books as well. Should not these be free? In addition to the Church, how do they make *Holy Water?* Isn't water...um, water? What is so holy about it? The Priest just says, "I bless thee" over the water... What makes him so *powerful?* This is the same religion, which was deeply investigation over many generations for child molestation. Why are people continuing to believe such lies?

I was always under the impression that church & religious organizations, were merely *non-profit*...? Do you really think that the money you are donating goes to God himself? Have you not noticed that various churches in California are driving around in a BMV or Benz? Funny, maybe I should work at a Church, instead of driving in my beat up 2002 rust bucket of a Ford Focus Wagon.

It is simple, a story created for *man* to be manipulated. It is hard to believe that the masters of the universe would stray *man* so far from learning and knowing the truth...

I understand that believing in a *Higher Power* is part of being a human. However, why would you put so much personal faith, into the hands of such an ongoing lie? I simply do not understand it.

About a decade ago, I went with my wife's father to Anaheim Stadium, in California. This was for new believers & current believers for Christianity. There must have been 50,000 people (give or take a few thousand), and many of the new believers, were invited out to the *field* to "join" the club - so-to-speak.

Just before that happened, I remember looking around me, and had noticed how many people were waving their hands up into the air, acting as if they were about to touch *their* God!

For me, I have often attempted to be like those people, trying to feel closer to my *Creator*.   However, I never had seen or heard from God. Assured, there are many *signs* in our "bubble" of life. However, who has to say, that these signs came from God? Perhaps, these signs were merely sent from the Universe...

Nothing will change I understand that. This lie will keep "religious believers" gliding thru life, as if they

are somehow connected with *Their God*.
Nevertheless, isn't it ironic when many
of these same people who are blinded by
the Religious standpoint, do not believe
in Extra-Terrestrial Life? Moreover,
these same people who put full Trust &
Faith into their Governments - thinking
they had never been lied to...on
purpose. Please forgive me if I just
made you a bit irritated or angry, but
its total fact, not Fiction!

Chapter 2 - The Media

Haven't you ever wondered what happened to opening up the newspaper - which is going extinct - or even looking on the internet, it's all about gossip or sports, or even the latest, so-called wars?

Every time I review the news on Yahoo!, the first three slides - - has to do with these categories:

* Gossip, celebrities, the wars, politics, or terrorists.

Then as you look through the other 25-30 slides, they often carry unnecessary junk. That is not news. This is to cover up what is actually happening globally, to stray folks like you and me from what is actually happening daily.

You mean to tell me, with the billions of people on Earth, there is not something that is more qualified to be news...like the made-up gossip that is a daily news reading.

How about a new strain of virus we should be more concerned about, starving or dying people around the world, is this not news anymore?

Or what about the folks that live in Africa, that seems to be news to me, such as the Race or Diamond war, that has been reoccurring there since I've been alive...just because it's old news, doesn't mean we shouldn't have this be reinserted into our news, here in America. I get a kick out of the news...journalism is not what it used to be, that's for sure.

What about all of these reality shows? What happened to television? Man, you cannot even watch music videos on cable television anymore! You people have such a fascination with everyone else, other than yourself.

Sure, other people seem interesting at times, but not enough to make a whole season about it...have you ever seen that movie, *Ed TV*.

When did normal people, who are willing to do, everyday things - just in front of camera - become celebrities...just because they are on television.

I constantly get irritated when the media does show certain *offenses* for crime. How often do you see something about another *White* Police Officer killing an innocent unarmed *African-American?* It seems to be like the *Rodney King Beating* all over again. Here is another prime example, another African-American robbing a convenient store. Most normal minded folks, should realize by now, it most likely were a black person (sorry, African-American), but our so-called government wants us to fear Black People...why is that? I thought that we had laws for Racial Slander. Why should they get away with this?

The same could be said for showing on television, making fun of the Arabic man or woman behind the cash register, but hey who am I to judge?

Then when there are hate-crimes occurring, nothing is done about it in a just manner. Just to make the mob outside the court houses pleased with results, they generally just pick up a *stray* and place blame on that individual - not ever committing a crime in their life - and yet, all of a sudden, the media has all these allegations against such an individual, just to make various people satisfied.

Another thing that truly drives me up the wall is the no name various school shootings around our country - for example, the Sandy Elementary shooting. I apologize, but it seemed staged to me, especially since just weeks before the incident occurred, President Obama was trying to strike down on Gun Control Laws. Then when he was getting nowhere on the subject, we all of a sudden had a no-name school shooting? Then one of the mothers' a month later, was standing behind the President about enforcing Gun Control Laws, and people all over, agreed? What a manipulation! It sounds like somebody was paid off to me!

Not to mention, they shut down the so-called school permanently to destroy it, and build a new one...um, that sounds a bit fishy...Especially when the Columbine shooting happened, they didn't tear it down for a new one, they remodeled, and moved on.

Chapter 3 - The U.S. & Digital Age

I have mentioned this a few times in my previous books, the United States government is the biggest manipulator of all time...aside from the Pope.

They have lied to the American citizen's repeatedly. They even have this thing called a *Voting* system. What is the purpose? Everything is going digital, and computerized. Doesn't it simply defeat the purpose of cheating so easily?

Bush proved my theory on that one. They generated the numbers at the polls...dead or alive. It used to be a hole-punch card, then they went to coloring in the circles next to the candidate's name, now digital? Ha, go figure.

Think about this, majority of the Casino's nowadays; have made their slot machines digital. It has a computer program chip inside the slot machine. Moreover, you do not even put cash in the machine anymore. Many casinos are using a rechargeable card (similar to a rechargeable gift card).

The program inside the machine is programmed to keep taking your money, little by little, only to give you a small amount back. The purpose of this is to make you think that you are working up for the BIG win! In reality, you will lose more money this way, than gaining any back, or even get further ahead. Unless, you have figured out the best times of the day to show up for the big jackpot to be released, you may have well quit playing these *New & Improved* slot machines.

It is not any different from generating votes in the computers. People think that they are helping on choosing the newest candidates for President or Senator's even, or anyone else for that matter. However, the reality is, is that majority of these candidates were already picked to be placed into office. Haven't you watched the television series, *"House of Cards," it* explains it in that show...I knew about it when I was in high school?

Just like now, we have President Obama in charge...he is a democrat; the next President will be a Republic - I ALMOST GUARENTEE YOU OF THIS! Your votes will not matter, because this unknown candidate - that we may not even have heard of, before the election.

For example, such as Obama, who was already chosen long before the elections to replace the previous President! Yet, I would have to say 90% of American's still have not realized this yet!

This is another form of Manipulation. If you don't believe me, do your own research, every other new president, is a Republican, then the next one, will be a Democrat, it's always rotating, research and learn, pay attention during the campaigns! It is a rarity of two in a row, being Democrat or Republican. You have been informed.

Chapter 4 - Unnecessary Consumption

A sales representative sells his product daily, to people who do not necessarily need the product he is told to sell. Yet, this salesperson - and many like him - manipulate consumers into purchasing products they do not need or want all. This is Sales Manipulation, and some know it as, *The Power of Manipulation.*

Do you know how much wealthier we would all be, if we did not purchase some product we didn't need - or at one point - didn't even want?

Another good example:

When you are awaiting your tax

return deposits, you come to terms with a budget, most likely to pay off your current debt.

Then suddenly, the one who is stuck home, due to the recession, meanwhile your spouse is working their asses off, you noticed your account just got heftier. You received a windfall of money from your government.

You try to try, and try not to spend any obscene money while your other half is off to work, while you are staring at that balance. You have no vehicle to spend this money on; meanwhile, you are just a click away to spending it all online!

You start purchasing small stuff,

such as music, DVD's, and possibly clothes. Then you get more interested in the bigger, cooler stuff - for example, a new computer; or a laptop; or even a printer, etc. Before you know it, one or two, or even three simple purchases turn out to be hundreds to thousands of dollars, with only a few simple clicks.

Meanwhile, while you are pacing back and forth in your home, your significant other walks in from a long day at work, not knowing all the damage you have caused, because you could not wait to spend it on all on the things you do not need. You just were swooped in, for the *ALMIGHTY PURCHASE*! Now, you have an argument to face, and trust me, you will lose!

After trying to win that long drawn argument, your spouse decides to use the last forty or so dollars on a long deserved meal, that somebody else can cook and clean up.

Then, when the dust starts to settle in, that drawn out debt, is stacking up, and you cannot return any unnecessary purchases! I call this *Unnecessary Consumption.*

This all started due to the brochure you had received in your mailbox that morning, or a commercial ad you saw online, or even your TV while you were sipping on your morning brew.

These were all created by the *Masterminds of Manipulation,* and they are too damn good at their jobs!

This is widely known to happen too many. Moreover, it is all part of a *Global Manipulation. The purpose is for* widespread consumption...for products you do not need.

Believe me, when I express myself on this topic, commercial ads are truly, by far, the biggest manipulations of modern times, merely meant for you to waste your money, only to make these companies richer than they already are. In addition, what happened to word of mouth? Isn't that what *Twitter & Facebook* are meant for?

Not to say that all these items you just purchased, were unnecessarily items you did not need. However, entering into a store or thereby even purchasing things online, there will always be those annoying impulse purchases. Which then leave your pockets high & dry from your most recent shopping spree. Meanwhile, knowing damn well, you have to pay your mortgage or rent, or even that over-priced Utility bill sitting your kitchen table, you go from satisfied, to angry in a single heartbeat!

Now if you only had mastered *SELF-CONTROL*, you would have been able to pay off your current debt; and paying ahead, instead of falling behind even further!

Chapter 5 - Gas Price Industry

When I was growing up, my parents had told me, that when they received their Driver's License's - back in the late 1970's - the price of gasoline was marked down to seventy cents per gallon.

When I grew up, and received my Driver's License, I was paying $1.02 for the cheap stuff. If I had a kid at 18, he/or she would be paying $2.49 a gallon for the cheap stuff. Perhaps, it was in the past 2 years when it was over-priced. It stayed at an extremely crazy price, $4+ per a gallon.

Let me get this straight, from the time my parents started paying for their gas to the time I started putting gas in my own car (or theirs), it was only a thirty cent difference. Why in the hell did it sky rocket so out of control? I know damn well the oil companies have been lying to us about an oil shortage, they have storage lockups for that... Why all of a sudden, in just under a century, of selling gasoline, did these trillion airs get so damn greedy? Is a trillion dollars not enough? How much money will it take, before enough is enough? While they are driving around in their million dollar sports cars daily - seven or less m.p.g. - we are all taking it up our rumps! Moreover, we are losing money all the while; they are robbing us of our money!

Chapter 6 -

Manipulation can be a Dangerous Game

When I see various companies, governments, media, various individuals, and yes, even the oil companies using manipulation to receive something - generally money - it truly gets under my skin - if you have not noticed by now.

I get frustrated, that so many people do not know how to avoid these brainwashing & manipulative methods, that are constantly being used daily. Honestly, I can tell you from my own personal experience, which it has taken me years to learn how to avoid these manipulations, and there are still many situations, where I have found myself being _**Lured in by the Big Bad Wolves**_ to be consumed!

I have come to the realization that it is not any different from learning to control your temper, or change your negative thoughts & energy into a positive flow, and even a positive outlook on life. This helps a great deal to stray from these horrific manipulators.

Life has many varieties on the planet we are all living on...Earth. There is so much more to life than being dragged down, held back, or be surrounded by negativity.

My point is that when you have

extra money, you are starring at your debts, and you know you will need that extra 10+ dollars, do not spend it on something you do not need. Of course, you spend it on entertainment we all need that. Many choices include books, movies, games, theme parks, museums, historical sites, and so much more, its fine to an extent. However, your bank account is not screaming at you to drain it empty.

Trust me, I have been struggling myself, life is not easy. Especially, when everything we need to survive in life, keeps being raised. Milk, food, vegetables, meats, coffee, smokes, alcohol, medicine...oh geez

medicine...another overprice rip off,
that we need!

The average human is not rich by
any means after the most recent
Recession. My wife and I had descent
credit just before that B.S., had
started. I remember that we were ahead
in all of our bills, we had hardly any
outstanding debt, and we were able to
enjoy the pleasures of life. Our credit
score was pushing 700.

After everything went to shit, it
is 415-420. That credit score does not
even get you a payday loan! Ha, ha,
ha...jokes on us right.

Majority of us, are in fact, on a
strict budget. So strict, in fact, that

we can barely survive on the money we earn each week. Nevertheless, just over the top, where we do not get easy handouts! Therefore, that extra money we feel we have to spend - because we heard an ad or saw one - does not mean we actually do. Ignore it.

Shut the television or radio off. Get away from the internet. Read a book, go for a walk, spend time with your family, play a game, hell write a book, and create a magnificent piece of art! I guarantee you, that there is something at your home - inside or out - that you already have, that you do not necessarily have to be swindled into purchasing.

Do not fall into the trap of consumption. If you want to read, buy a cheap book or get one from your local library, or even off Kindle. Do not go get that expensive television in the store you do not want to wait until Black Friday to get!

Chapter 7 - Hollywood

Have you ever noticed the subliminal messages in various movies or even music? I have. Moreover, I hope you have, too.

I have often wondered about how the United States of America, had even landed on the Moon, when Spaceship, after Spaceship had failed so many times. Perhaps, our Government had asked Hollywood to portray it, as if we went into space...

I have watched that video of the spaceship leaving Earth so many times, and Lance Armstrong taking *Man's First Step* repeatedly. The more I watch it, the more it looks like something

Hollywood could have easily replicated.

Were you there? No. You were at home,

watching your black & white television.

How hard would it have been to replicate

the Voyage to the Moon? For Hollywood,

it would have come easy. For you and

me, it would have been impossible.

I have also found that in certain

movies, such as *The Transformers Series,*

that there was a variety of subliminal

messages. Perhaps, the aliens are

staying in hiding, on the *dark side* of

the Moon. Not to mention the movie,

Contact. If you watch those movies, pay

attention to the messages, it is not as

farfetched as you may have initially

thought. You probably walked away from watching these movies saying, "Man that was an awesome movie, but I'm sure glad it didn't happen".

How would you even know if it happened? Do you really think our Government would come clean with something so extraordinary? The answer to that question is simple...nope.

If you want proof from that theory, well think back to Roswell in 1947. Then a few days after the incident, they interchanged their story, saying it was a weather balloon. They love using that lie. Not to mention, how many times have we all heard this lie repeatedly? "It was a training exercise."

If those two lies were not bad enough, you have reality television shows, to help blind us with those bullshit lies.

For example, you have "U.F.O. Hunters", "Ancient Aliens," and so much more. These two shows crack me up. They start so damn fascinating, and then they encourage the lies, by discriminating the truth. Making out an incredible witness, sound like hacks. Then, proving *their* theory of *The Weather balloon!*

Section 2

Focus, Do not Look Away!

Chapter 1

Do you remember that scene from the last *Terminator* movie...? The dude who truly thought he was a man, only later, he came to the realization, that he was in fact, a robot (or a machine as they put it).

Who has to say, that we may not be the same way, when it comes to Alien-hybrids? One would never know, right?

Majority of our population would either roll their eyes at this book, or be interested in reading on.

Personally, if you want to think for yourself, as a superior individual,

I recommend you to continue reading, just to hear me out!

Is the concept far off from the truth? I do not think so, not one bit. Consider this. Why would our World Leaders cover up every single Alien encounter that has ever happened here in the United States, or any other country on our Globe? Why would they have covered up the incident in Roswell so quickly?

Be assured, for many people, Aliens could very well be a scary thing to come across. Why would we perceive this idea of an Alien invasion, to be so full of fear? For me, the concept is not that far stretched. It isn't just something

70

out of the movies either, now is it?

Our country, and even the rest of the world is filled with deception, and many *normal* and *abnormal* citizens realize this. The 21st century became a revelation all across the globe. In addition, many people are starting not only question the methods of our so-called *Leaders*, but Religion as well.

Did you see all those hits on *UTube*, for the video of one of the Agents standing in the background with President Obama? If you looked closely, the man seemed to be a man, until you paid more closely to the detail. It seemed to be, as if this being was in fact, a shape-shifter.

71

The reality we perceive has been a mysterious wonder to me, just as many realists as I am certain. With the B.S. taught in school about human history, I found it to be more of an irony, than a historical fact. To me, it was just like reading the *Bible* - which for me, is a book filled with lies!

If I still don't have you convinced the similarities of humanity vs. aliens, then consider this, our D.N.A.'s do not exactly match up with Gorilla's or Apes. Darwin's theory of man was merely a theory. These variety of theories, can quite possibly lead to truth, sure, but still, only a theory.

Recently, I had to explain to my

cousin, that the Non-Fiction category of books of theories, is still considered NON-FICTION...a theory can simply be a theory. However, if a theory can land in our historical books, then why would it be considered fiction? At first glance, many theories - even my own at times - could be, and would be considered to be more or less, fictional. If you pitch it just right and everyone who reads into the theory, it can be believable, such as religion, right.

If Religion is solely based on Jesus Christ's resurrection, and him dying on the cross for people's sins, and "we" as a people in modern times, then Religion is also a theory. It is written to deceive man in my opinion, however, it is a believable story that can blind or stray humanity from truth. Either way, it is a story. How is it any different from my story, my theory? It is still opinionated...right?

Now, with all of that being said, and out in the open - how is it that in modern times, with all of our latest technologies, we still believe in *Darwin's Theory?*

Life is a mystery - human life and all the life that surrounds us. Evolution is also a mystery. However, when I think back to what I was taught in school, to what I know now. I believe that my theory of us being hybrids of Aliens, it is not farfetched at all...I am certain of this.

Before my father passed on to his next life, we got to talking about several topics. Nevertheless, the one in particular has stuck with me for the past 9 years, since his passing in August of 2006 - this includes, "how humans actually arrived on Earth", and, "how many believe in Religion". Also how the Dinosaurs once roamed the earth, and then all perished, during this asteroid strike.

What if the asteroids that landed on Earth all those years ago, were not actually asteroids as our *Great Thinkers* once had thought....

What if, these asteroids were actually in fact Space Ships, which were shooting down, killing all of the dinosaurs *they* had thought to be harmful to our species?

In the movies, we have had watched numerous stories on Alien encounters, Alien warfare vs. man, and we have seen various movies on Dinosaurs. This day and age, if we did come from another planet that was dying, how does it differ from the plot of *Transformers?* These various movies have more truth in them than you may realize.

Chapter 2

I have found others and myself like me, to have the fascination of looking up into the sky. Not just to take a quick glance at the stars, but knowing that deep down, I came from somewhere else. Not me personally of course, but humans in general. I often notice things that others around me do not quite see yet. Perhaps I was designed differently, perhaps there is many of what ifs, but the bottom line, is that I believe this to be true. I am not crazy, but at times, I feel as if I am alone.

If it were not for me helping my wife to look at our world a bit differently than how she was raised, I sure would feel even more alone. I see things that I know majority of our population does not quite see, and maybe I am the only one. However, it could also be that nobody discusses this. Moreover, we feel scared even to discuss this. I am not sure, but I still feel alone, until I start to listen to people like *Eminem*.

I know deep down, he may feel like me, as to we have many of the same views. Other musicians that come to mind are *Rhianna, Katy Perry,* and a few others. They talk about aliens a lot in their lyrics. Perhaps it is merely a story that sounds good as a song, or it is they trying to help our civilization learn that we are not alone after all.

I for one have known this to be true since I was a little kid. I know my father had felt the same way. My father once read a book, explaining the possibility of our World Leaders meeting with extra-terrestrial life. Unfortunately, he never told me the rest of what the book was about, and I never found the book he read this is. I wish my father lived longer, and chose to stay on Earth a bit longer, as his final mission in life, was to commit suicide, and accomplished it. However, he was a

lot like me in a sense & he had felt
alone. Unfortunately, he did not
receive the love when he was a young
buck, and it he was lost throughout his
life, because of it.

To an extent, I felt his misery, as
I had this closeness to him, that nobody
else had shared.

Chapter 3

A theory of mine, of man possibly being Alien-hybrids, could really be possible. Some of us have different perspective of life. Such as, out living our parents, out doing our family, changing our belief systems half way through our lives, and rising up. Showing our stars & stripes is not going to cut it. We live in a world with such negativity & deception, that it feels so difficult to change.

I grew up in a household that was in constantly negative & criticizing conditions, such as most. I was criticized & still felt like the outsider - in my own family. It feels as if I was adopted, to be honest with you. I have very little traits of my Mother & my sister. I had felt like living in that household, that I was being held back. Perhaps, this is the exact reasoning, why I started my writing career so damn late in my life.

Lately, I have been on a writing rampage. I have achieved five paperbacks and this book will be my sixth. I have been busy in changing my stripes in the family, and I know I will achieve greatness from doing so. Therefore, I cannot change certain circumstances.

Knowing things as I became older would have helped me achieve earlier goals in my life. If I knew these things rolling around in my head now, and applied them to when I was younger, I would have been writing books, since I graduated from High School, back in 1998! However, that is not how life is meant to be... If only I can use a time machine!

Our lives are filled with challenges, discrimination, opinions, fear, and finally achievement. To achieve something, is personally, the best feeling an individual can accomplish. However, getting there, well that my darlings, are filled with

challenges, and negativity from others.
Not just family and the possibility of
your friends; but the evil throughout
the world.

As you get older in life, you learn
about the cosmic way of life. A balance
we come to learn, known as *Good vs.*
Evil. It is just the way of life, and
it does not end here with Earth.

Chapter 4

As various people in America have come to learn about the challenges in life, most of the working population has to start from the bottom up. I believe that the reasoning for this would be to spotting the next *Leaders* of achievement. Even athletes that are great, even have to start at the bottom of the mountain, just so they can reach the top of the mountain.   The only way to stand out is if you think & act differently.

In my case, I had stood out for years before entering High School; I just did not know it yet. I knew I was different to a certain extent, of course. However, I did not truly know what it meant. I didn't know this mainly because I when I lived with my family, I was told that I would just be working in a "day-to-day" job, or even living off of the government with S.S.I. - due to my born with, disability.

I was told not to have big dreams or achieve greatness. This was on the daily in my home. I know majority of poverty is, and always will be, forced into hearing and learning this. However, this needs to change.

Various musicians that turned out to be great, and become the highest achievers in their field, actually grew up in poverty. Such as musicians like Eminem, Tupac, and that's just the tip of the iceberg. If this were the case, is this simply a challenge from our Universe?

Our Universe sends us *signals & signs* all of the time. Majority of religious believers think these same signals & signs are from their *Gods*.

Man wrote the Bible, just as they made up Religion. I have said this previously, but if you look at an old painting of J.C.'s mother while being pregnant; there is a U.F.O. in the background, with light shining down to Mary's stomach. As if it were saying,

90

"we made her pregnant!"

If Aliens were a mythical story, such as Greek mythology, then why has there been so many various paintings on canvas and cave walls throughout history? Not to mention the millions of eyewitness testimonies around the globe today?

If Canadians were as honest as I hear, then why is the rest of the world around them so ignorant? Ignorance is a sure sign of deception, is it not?

I truly believe in extra-terrestrial life. I have often dreamed about meeting one someday, whether it is this lifetime or my next - if I have not already...but I am not going into that!

If the next part of my life is being in another life form, I can almost guarantee you that it will be on another planet, let alone a completely different galaxy. In addition, it could very well be quite similar to earth. Who knows? I do not. I am just merely speculating, as many do.

Who has to say that we will not end up living on another planet in our own solar system? Various people in the 20th century have even claimed to meet certain Martians from the planet, as we know as, Venus. Therefore, if it were true - and not a hoax - is not there much more to life, which the "big dogs"

92

are not relaying to the rest of humanity. In addition, if you read up on Ufologists, many of the great one's have perished. - Whether it be an "accidental" car crash, or "suicide". Therefore, if U.F.O.'s an Aliens were all a myth, why does our government and others throughout our planet, go to such extremes to kill people off to keep their big secret?

Chapter 5

If aliens came to our planet from the time the planet became livable, then why would they encourage our *Leaders* to cover this up? Shouldn't the truth stay out in the open?   We are taught that, "The truth shall set you free". If this were something we were taught growing up, from generation to generation, then whey is the world filled with such dishonesty and continuous, constant lies.

When our government is not satisfied with something that happened that fell from the sky, they make up a story saying, "It was a weather balloon." Why do they keep lying to us? Are they that fearful on how civilians will react? If so, what is their biggest fear about it? Is it something more elaborate about these pressing lies & cover-ups they do not want to reveal. I believe that there is a bigger picture here, and that is what is being covered up. In addition, since we have lived with these lies, we all run when we hear something crazy on the radio, such as when *The War of the Worlds* was first played on live radio. From what the articles say, *we all scattered like ants in pure panic & chaos!*

Since we are filled with deception

on the daily, we are also filled with fear in return. Why is this so important for the Government to hang over us? What is so important to them, that they have to hide from us? We as a nation, supposedly pay taxes for these said lies. It seems like the United States of America is no different from that of the Roman Empire some centuries ago! Explain to me the difference, because I do not see any...

Back to the hybrids vs aliens; why is this concept so farfetched? We have a ton of conspiracies floating around on the internet these days, and many of the conspiracies makes a ton of sense. Not to mention, great movies!

Generally, some conspiracies that are well thought out become deleted from Homeland Security (or some other three-letter agency).

If these so-called conspiracies are just theories, then why is the *Hand* from our Governments striking down so swiftly? What do they fear to happen?

Geez, I thought the normal person, just glances at things like *conspiracies* and then moves on with their day, such as gossip from tabloids...

Let me get this straight. When the general population thinks of Aliens, the first picture they get into their heads, are these little green men? Wasn't that the propaganda from Hollywood? You do realize that the *Green Men* you picture in your head was in fact created in Hollywood first...right.

Just like humanity, they have different races, just as aliens do. I have first-hand experience in witnessing a few different races.   Unlike the other, I became fearful of my life, expecting harm and rage. Whether this was my instincts or from my upbringing, I cannot tell you. Either way, they looked completely different, even though their spaceships were quite similar.

The race of aliens that seems to me that everyone fears is known to be *The*

Greys. I am uncertain of the term for the other race, but they truly resembled sparkly, tall elves. They were about 8-10 feet in height, with sparkles to their white skin. They have long fingernails, and beautiful wavy, blonde hair. In which, they only have hair on their heads, and nowhere else.

I did my own stint of research online, just to try and located what other people have come across over time. However, I never did find that particular race as a specification.

In another case of my research, I had stumbled on something of strangeness, and it made sense after looking deeper into it. The name that it is known is

Agartha. It was to be believed, that there is an underground living space, underneath land & ocean here on Earth. I believe the race I had encountered last year, and even before that even - came from there, after their planet was destroyed. And I also believe - which many others share this theory as well - that it is a place for moving from one planet to another, or even one dimension to another; possibly thru a teleportation machine or something else, that none of us has ever encountered.

When looking into this myth-like story, you will eventually find out that the openings to enter and/or exit from this *living space* are in fact, *No Fly*

Zones. Now, why would you have no fly
zones in those same zones of entry to
this underground layer? In addition to
all of this, you can find a drawing of a
map - which tells me that a human has
most certainly came back alive - and it
shows in full detail, that it is
actually underground, as I had
previously stated. It shows that it is
at least 200 miles below the Earth's
physical surface. Here is what lies
above the key points of the map, which
we are aware:

- Admiral Byrd's Flight 1947

- Kentucky Mammoth Cave

- the *Test* site for the Atomic

Bomb

- Mt. Epomeo Italy

- Pyramid of Giza

- Dero Caves (with stolen
  saucers)

- Center of gravity - 400 miles
  inward

- Brazil

- Mato Grosso

In the middle of the map, it shows
the name, "Land of Advanced Races". It
shows different sections of advanced
races, and it even has mountains inside

their little world. In addition, in the center it has a picture of a sun (Central Sun). If that were to be in fact, the truth, and not some man made story, then their sun, would be *Earth's Core*, wouldn't it be?

If this were to be a true existing place of origin here on earth, why is it not known? There aren't any movies or documentaries on it? What is the harm of learning about this place? I know I would like to know more...However, only various humans are even allowed to enter those sites. I have even come across old entries about being killed in these areas, by various groups affiliated with the *WORLD LEADERS* who have been keeping a close eye on this particular site.

We have actual, factual proof that we live with Aliens. They come out of hiding from time to time, probably for resources, as we do. We all need food, and I am sure they do.

If Admiral Byrd's Flight of 1947 did occur, why wasn't it in newspapers all around the world? Why did it not get publicity, as it should have, truth or fiction? I believe the possibility of the events could be truthful, but again, the World Leaders that we have, who we may never actually see or read about, do not want this knowledge to be in our society. It is just that simple. It is politics. Just as why we have

Cryptic animals washing up on our beaches occasionally. It hits the news, and then all of a sudden, it becomes a cover up, a scientific experiment gone wrong. It is always something.

There are many variables to the fiction and facts here on Earth. Just as, *We're not alone* or ghosts, or religions, there are so many unexplained events, and occurrences on earth, that the truth will never be reviled, as the ones who seem to discuss this open mindlessly, generally will end up in an Asylum. I would not be one bit surprised if I were forced into one...I just hope that does not happen!

Chapter 6

How many of you, have witnessed a U.F.O.? Did you know there has been millions of siting is throughout our planet? Did you also know, that N.A.S.A. has special workers to edit the *live* photography or video feed that they receive from their satellites to erase these Alien spaceships? Kind of makes ya wonder why does not it. In addition, if you contact your local Air Force base, they generally create a lie, to make yourself more at ease, do not them... Many times, they also tell you - at a later date - that they were testing a new aircraft, or it was just a

weather balloon! In any case, do not
believe what the Air Force tells you,
and in addition, do not bother reporting
to any U.F.O. website saying that they
will look into your findings. Because
in the end, they will say, "The evidence
that you gave us, is inconclusive." I
have had that one back in January of
2015, and then found out in May of 2015,
that they in fact, had worked secretly
with the Government. I've had that from
the last time I attempted in reporting
(with exclusive evidence of a U.F.O.) my
claims, and within weeks, I had four
different - blacked out (with limo
tinted windows) Suburban's or Yukon's
following me for a month! I live in an

area where *they* have to fly in from another "sector".

Here is an interesting thing I located in my research about U.F.O. siting's, in the 1950's in Washington D.C., there was a time when there were many U.F.O.'s spotted over the White House & Capital building. If you were to search Google, all you have to do is type in, *The Real Majestic 12 & Harry Truman's 1950 Washington D.C., U.F.O. meeting.*

After the closing of the *Majestic-12 Project*, several more groups that are secret had been formed... such as, *Skull & bones Scroll & Key*.

Six of the original Majestic 12 members were in those other two groups mentioned. Majority of the members were graduates from Yale & Harvard University, but not all of course.

At the end of 1979, the Grey's started inserting probes inside their human abductees' brains. The reason for this particular experiment was to try to control their "test subjects". Of course, they later failed, as it caused life-threatening symptoms.

Later on, it was discovered by humans, that the Grey's purpose, were in fact, attempting to perform "*genetic cross-breeding*" on various human, female abductees.

This was breaking the Grey's "Treaties & Agreements" with both the United States & the Soviet Union. The U.S. & the U.S.S.R. have been secret allies since 1983. In part, they created a secret weapon for protection against the Grey's; the name ironically was *Star Wars*.

During the years with President Ronald Reagan, another Ultra Secret Project was initiated; it was to be named, "Project Zeus".

Project Zeus' weapons were pointed directly towards the sky, towards space. These gnarly weapons were to produce hurling lasers & particle beams of lightning bolts! *We* had sent out into space "deflectors" or "mirrors" that would reflect these beams back down to Earth in various locations, of the Grey's military bases. Both of the Grey's main military bases were being the United States of America & the Soviet Union.

There are various books written in the 1980's about on-going affairs that took place. Authored by *General Graham,* entitled "The Higher Frontier." Another Author, *Stefan Possony,* with Co-Author, *Jerry Pournelle,* entitled, "The Strategy of Technology".

Apparently, at the end of President Ronald Reagan's term, he had mentioned his famous *Star Wars* speech & labeled

it, "The Strategic Defense Initiative".
He also mentioned to the public, the
possibilities of hostile E.T.'s. In
addition, he did not elaborate the
extremity of how harmful these creatures
could be of course, because he did not
want panic on his hands. I believe he
tested "the people" that day, and many
were not really considering the
intensity of his thinking process.

However, if such weapons were ever
actually used to shoot into these so-
called *mirrors*, they would have
annihilated everything in sight,
including human cities that surrounded
these bases. Which in turn, would be
hundreds of miles, if not thousands, if

114

both weapons were ever to be fired.

The satellites that carried these *mirrors* were disguised as SDI Tracking & Data Relay Satellites. In which, were sent into orbit in 1984 by NASA, who did not know the actual purpose of these satellites, but launched it into orbit, regardless.

Another Project named, *Project Aquarius,* was originated from *Project SIGN.* The project was responsible for collecting all scientific, technological, medical, and intelligence information. The data collected from this project was used to present *Stealth Technology.* However, after 1969, this project was terminated, along with

Project Grudge & Bluebook.

From Project Aquarius, came Project Plato. It was established for the purpose including diplomatic relations with Aliens.

In a secured section of the C.I.A. headquarters in Langley, Va., remains files from Majestic 12 & many other closed out, Top Secret Projects, known as *"The Bible"*. The Bible holds various reports & accounts on aspects of Alien visitation. It also reveals all members of these various Projects, which started with President Harry Truman.

Here is a fun fact for all you that follow U.F.O. hunters around the globe.

U.F.O. investigator Bill Moore was actually recruited by the C.I.A. In 1988, Bill Moore, allegedly became an Agent of Operation Majestic-12, and had been *Planted* in the civilian U.F.O. movement to help misguide & confuse other U.F.O. researchers. It would explain why he does not necessarily release factual truth in his magazine or any television related shows. Haven't you ever noticed, that he generally answers a question followed with another question?

In the late 1980's, many satellites were launched into space. In which, started to make the Grey's suspicious.

These were all on various websites,

which included

www.bibliotecapleyades.net/ &

www.wikipedia.com/

Whether you believe these stories or not, there has been numerous ex-employees that had worked at Area 51 or even S4 - which is the Grey's military base just south of Area 51 - that had come out with their testimonies, and many of these same various people, generally end up dead after speaking out. Not all of course, but most. I assure you, this is not coincidental.

If you had a huge secret, that could affect your very well-being, what would you do if that secret came to *Public Knowledge?* Would you kill for

118

it? As it happens, people do. As messed up as it sounds to a regular civilian, our government and many other governments, do in fact kill people to keep their secrets hidden away from regular people all of the time. If these people is not killed, however, they most likely lose all credibility and are never heard from again...which makes me believe they were thrown in some shit-hole jail cell for life, or mental institute!

Going back a bit to Agartha, I forgot to mention that a few select people from around the globe, has in fact, been accepted by these Aliens that live there. In addition, both the North & South Pole are the main entrances from Air-Flight.

If you do run across a map (typically a drawn out map); you will see that many various caves throughout our world, all lead down into their world. If this is the case, then why am I just learning of this now?

If you further your investigation,

such as I did, you will also learn that
Agartha was created, some 25,000 years
ago. Why isn't this something known to
modern times? Why are there so few
books written? What is so wrong with
our world today, which things that are
created with such mystery & beauty are
constantly covered up by humans in *High
Power?*

Chapter 8

    If you decided to make a visit to

this website,

www.bibliotecapleyades.net/, you can

learn all sorts of new things. Such as,

the history of the human race; what we

still haven't yet learned; how our race

is confused about how "we" as a people -

who are religious - see's our God as a

physical being, instead of something,

somehow attached to our inner soul.

    Another great thing you can learn

at that website address is the various

main races of Aliens. How they have

affected humans throughout past &

present times. In addition, how our civilization keeps hiding the factual truth from the rest of the population.

You will also learn of a Speaker named, Germane. This *Germane* figure is in fact an alien speaking to various members of a secret society, so high up in power, which literally, only few people are aware. These secret societies are most likely - in my personal opinion - are probably our *Actual Earth Rulers*, not the modern day Presidents, or even the Kings & Queens that remain in the world.

Chapter 9

Since we had elected President
Obama, we've had a ton more conspiracies
rise in our hidden networks on the
backside of the internet. One of my
favorites happen to be how some
conspirators had assumed that President
Obama is a Reptilian...

At first, it made me giggle I will
not lie. Nevertheless, after much
consideration, after learning of all of
the different various species of Aliens
in the past four years, it would not
surprise me one bit at this point in my
life. It would in fact, make perfect

sense. Who knows, except Obama himself
& others that closely work with him!

I mean if you look at all the Alien
stuff out there, the more realistic
conspiracies, it absolutely, would make
perfect sense to have a Reptilian-hybrid
acting out as a President of one of the
most powerful countries of all
time...would it not? It would make
things run more smoothly for that race,
depending on what they are trying to
keep covered.

Consider all of the things
President Obama tried to take away from
the American People - gun control being
one of them. That seemed to be his top
priority of banning Americans to bear

arms since he has been the acting President. It is starting to calm down, since he only has about a year left, but for the first 5ish years of office, that was his main agenda...aside from the lame ass *Obama Care Act!*

It brings me to another "food for thought" for all of you to reconsider. Think back during the J.F.K. days; now think about why he was assassinated. He was Washington D.C.'s man in charge, and he was going to turn into a Whistle-blower. The C.I.A. new this and many various other agencies did as well. The various many assassinations that had taken place on many of our Presidents, and somebody during that time killed the

President. If it was an outside job,
don't ya think they would have killed
somebody that was a good President?
Like Truman or the past few Bush's? Now
why would somebody plan such a strategic
assassination for John F. Kennedy? He
was not only the youngest President I
think that our country ever had, but
also the most intelligent! In addition,
when he said, "We for the people", he
actually had meant it!

    I do not know about the rest of
you, but there are many various "facts"
in history that just do not add up.
Such as the proclaimed assassination
with all of our Presidents that date,
back to even Lincoln.

When you look at the Presidents
that was not killed, who were not
running our nation the way *the people*
had seen fit, why was there such a gap
in such assassinations?

Section 3:

My Personal Accounts

Chapter 1

Throughout my life, I have experienced a ton of strange encounters. Many may not believe me, but I have had my share of strangeness from this planet, we call home.

For starters, I have had my share fare of U.F.O. sightings, to a few occasions of Extra-Terrestrial beings, to things that literally have shown me they have come from Hell and other dimensions on Earth. I have had conversations with some, and I have found myself fleeing the scene from other encounters, as I am sure some of you may have.

In the 1990's, my family and I had lived in sunny California for about 15 years. It was beautiful, it was spectacular, and for a while, I witnessed things that I only thought were from books, and/or movies.

For starters, I would like to tell you that I am partially psychic. I have in the past have been able to be communicative with the past on, loved ones; and that was great for a while.

The problem is that being Psychic opens you up to everything paranormal...at least when you pursue into it.

I have seen demonic forces climbing my walls when I was only in eighth

grade. I started to experience
depression, due to the passing of my
Grandfather. It took about a year or
two to hit me, and when it did, I
somehow "clicked" something in my brain,
to experience a completely new level of
dimension beings.

I saw many bad things when I was
living with depression. It got to a
point, where I saw too much of what I
did not know at the time, how to *turn
off the power button!* Unfortunately,
this had led me to many suicide
attempts. Of course, as you all have an
understanding, that I was obviously
unsuccessful. Thankfully, I was.
Otherwise, I would not be writing you

this book today!

There was two times that had worked, and I was dead for two minutes on both accounts. During the time I was dead, I saw another new level. Many various people around the world - who have been said to have died, and then were sent back to earth - have had similar experiences.

In my experience, I saw a dark tunnel...this tunnel was pitch black dark. Then I saw the demons - from my bedroom wall - in a furious burning fire, and then I had experienced pain. This pain, I believe to be the pain from hurting those of whom were around me, such as my family & other loved ones. I think it may have been things I have once said (to hurt them) to the actions of attempting suicide or running away. After the pain, I floated to another section. The red fury was no longer around me, and I was sent back thru the dark corridor. Then at the end of this darkness, was a glowing orb of light. The light was so intense; it had filled me with love, peace, and harmony. I could not wait to move forward. I was shown all of my previous experiences, and then the possibilities of my future. There were many things that had come true (and some that have not yet), that I am currently waiting for. Like my first two science fiction novels to turn into movies. Going from being poor as hell, to rich that Don King! The other thing that has not happened yet is parenthood. As I may have mentioned early, I am 35, and my wife is 36. Which means if we don't have a child by 37-39, we won't even care about having a child at that point, because we'll be too old in our ages, by the time they graduate from High School, not to mention, college (if they attend).

It was a strange experience. I still remember that I was hovering above my body, being held in some sort of trance in the corner of the wall of the room (in 9th grade when the school doctors had to save my life). It was odd seeing my body still, and yet, I felt an ease. I saw my grandfather (who died three years before this experience), and I was thankful to be reacquainted with him. He showed me a book that I was to write over two decades later!

To say the least, the out-of-body experience when thinking you are passing on to whatever lies on the other side awaiting us, was mind changing!

Chapter 2

Not long after finishing tenth grade, I received my permit to start to learn how to drive. Many things at that point started to change for me, because my mood had changed. I was not experiencing things from *hell* and I was starting to come to terms with dealing with my grandfather being gone.

Sometime in my junior year, I received my Driver's License! It was literally like winning the lottery for me! I was no longer held down, and I can go out and have fun. My parents were starting to do better financially, and they helped me get my first car. It was not free - as if my sister's - and it still had meant a lot for me to get my first car. It was great until it started to fall apart on me, but it was a step in the right direction!

Since I was able to drive to places without supervision, I started driving to places that I probably should not have, but I did, to say the least. T

These places were mostly in what is known now as, *Rancho Santa Margarita.* During the time I first received my license and car, it was not a city yet, just a whole lot of dirt, with city streets. This was at the time, where many various young adults went to *Race* their cars. It was fun, but illegal!

When I was not trying to ruin my car by racing, I would go to secluded areas to stare into the sky above. This was away from the cities lights, and you could actually see the stars. There were few places where I lived, that you can actually see more than one star.

The first time I was out there, I saw a few U.F.O.'s passing throughout the night's sky. It was incredible. I did not give it much thought at the time, what the consequences would be, if these damn things actually landed. It never had crossed my mind, seeming how most of the ones I had seen, seemed like miles from me.

The first U.F.O. - in which I had

witnessed - was during my track time in early High School; I saw it stand still (so to speak), and then it went left to right, then straight up into the air towards space. It were as if it were putting on a show for me (there was not anybody near me who had saw this), but only me. Which even now, it seems strange that I was the only one who saw this object.

I remember telling my father about the first one I had saw, he was intrigued, but I was not sure if he took me serious. He was aware of my abilities of being Psychic, but I do not think he knew the extent of this.

Back to the other siting is at

hand. After *Rancho Santa Margarita* became a city, I was in search for a new area, since the cops in that city did not like poor kids driving around late at night!

I ended up doing a lot of driving near the closed *El Toro Marine Base*. The roads were generally secluded at nighttime, and there were few cops in the area, as you mostly had to deal with the left over Military Police. Considering the base was closed, it was used for many secret meetings. I saw many things happen there that I have not disclosed to anyone, and I will not start now.

Chapter 3

Moving on to 2001, my sister, and I had decided to drive from California to New York State (where we live now). It was the first time we had done anything that drastic with each other - I miss those times...

We left and it was the summer of 2001, and it was the greatest experience my sister and I had experienced together, maybe even more for me than her, even.

We went north going to Yellowstone & Yosemite National Park first, that was awesome. Then we went a bit further north, and drove to Mt. Rushmore. That was okay, it was a distance from where you can actually look at the mountain, but luckily, I had a camera (before the digital days) that I could zoom in to get a better look. I cannot wait to go back with the camera I have now!

From there we went east going the Dakota's (very boring scenery), then making our way to Washington D.C. It was a total pain in the ass to the White House when not being too familiar with the area. Unfortunately, they did not allow any tourists to enter in to the White House. Supposedly, there was construction going on, but after what happened on September 11, that year, I doubt it was for construction reasons!

We did not get to enjoy what D.C. had to offer, as to my gut; feeling (on September 10) said to leave fast!

My sister and I had stopped at the cemetery, and then saw the changing of the guards, and then I told her we should not spend another night as we planned. I told her I had a bad feeling, she listened, and we were off to New York. We got in late, and we stayed at one of her friends' apartment.

My sister woke me up early that next morning, and she was watching the planes hit the Twin Tower buildings, I thought she was watching a movie. Then I had noticed quickly that it was the news. I was shocked, as everyone around the country was.

Like many, we were glued to the television for hours. It must have been like that for the people who got the news of the *ASSINATION OF J.F.K.*

My wife had called me in a frantic, because we were actually going to go to New York City, and I talked my sister out of it, due to my gut feelings! Thank god, for those Gut feelings I get - quite frequently, I might add - otherwise, we would be dead from that too.

Chapter 4

After our 3,000-mile road trip, I thought we would never go on another one. It was over quickly, I flew back after the tragedy 9/11 year, and my sister stayed a bit longer. I was married, and I did not want to be away from her for another two weeks. It was hell flying back, and I had many *standbys* from the airline. Everyone was paranoid, and became on high alert with whom they were flying.

I still remember finally boarding in Buffalo; it took nearly four hours, as they had delay after delay. They had all planes grounded for four days during that time. I hit the bar like many, and was drunk by the time I entered the plane...bad idea...

After returning home, to California, my wife was so happy to see me, and thanked me for not visiting D.C. any longer - let alone NYC. That would have been a big mistake, and if it were not for my "feelings", I would have been dead years ago!

Nothing happened for my family or me during those years. It was quiet, and I began to party, as I was 21 at the time. I drank a lot, especially when I hit 22. My close friend had turned 21, and I somehow became his designated driver when we went out. In which, I

almost got a DUI if it wasn't for the
soon-to-be Retiring Cop that was
training a newbie, and was nice enough
to wait until I sobered up!

I happened to stop by the beach to
take a quick leak, and the cop just
mentioned, was waiting for me outside
near my car. It was a nice visit, and a
boring buzz, but I was able to walk away
without handcuffs!

I did not drink more than one or
two drinks after that night, when going
out with my friend. I did not want it
to be jinxed the *next* time. I was
pulled over a lot in CA, because I fit
their profile on gang-bangers and young
criminals. When they say they do not

discriminate criminals, they do. They actually look for new criminals in certain various areas in California, and push and push, until one day, when you do not have a record; you do, because they pushed you to it. Luckily, that wasn't me, I never got caught for my petty crimes (many of us have petty crimes we commit, just doing something stupid at the time, doesn't feel stupid or wrong until we get older!).

Either way, I was a partier when I was younger; I experienced a lot, most of which were hangovers! That part was not fun. My wife had her share too, but I will not go there!

I got sick of being led out of the

area near El Toro Marine base, and I
didn't want to be arrested (or something
worse) for seeing something I wasn't
supposed to. Therefore, I started going
to the beach after hours just to chill.
I cannot recall the name of the beach I
went to, but it was pretty secluded
except for the occasional young adult
couples getting it on!

I stayed near where the entrance
was, therefore, I wouldn't be too far
from booking out of there, if need be.

For a long period of time, nothing
substantial ever happened there. I
usually went there when I left my
friend's house. I used to spend the
night a lot at his house, but there was

a time, where I was not getting good sleep there anymore, it was caused to boredom.

One night, it was pushing two in the morning, and I felt uneasy on my walk down. I did not know why until I reached not far from the bottom. It was just before you enter the sand. I witnessed a small bomb fire, and at first, I thought it was a group of teens. Then all of a sudden, I heard a dog barking, it was a grizzly noise, not like a normal dog. Then I from the moonlight, I saw the dog. It was no Earthly dog, but it appeared to be a Hellhound. Not just one, but two, the beings with it, were not human either, I have not seen anything like them since, thankfully.

I never ran so fast to my car in my life. I still get chills when thinking back to that part in my life. It was the scariest moment I had, which I have had a few scary moments. Nevertheless, that was by far, the scariest.

That was the night I drove over 100 miles per hour. I got a ticket for 90! I passed by a cop alongside the freeway, in which another was coming onto the freeway, he pulled me over after I slowed down from 120...ha joke was on him. Ironically, the ticket was under two-hundred dollars...go figure!

Chapter 5

Moving on to 2004…

This was a bad year for me; I had a friend who got me back into Crystal Meth and other drugs. I was addicted, and I loved it in the beginning. This drug (when smoking it) was my kryptonite. It loved me, and I loved it. New York was my rehab… Which of course, as you figured, was partially the purpose of moving back to NY in 2006.

Anyways, when I was staying at my so-called friend's house during that phase, I became witness to many mysterious things once again.

I remember nearing the end of this *trip*, my friend had started to take notice what was happening underneath his trailer. His surrounding neighbors were using it as a heroin lab. He lived there close to three months, and never noticed it until we were using Meth! Go figure.

Once we had noticed, they did too. They started fighting back with us. First, there were scare tactics, followed by using bad methods from Voodoo. That with the trip we were on was not a good one. I did not really know what Voodoo was at the time, boy did I find out quickly. Luckily, my friend was a quick learner on how to use the defense magic used in this so-called religion.

There were 3-4 hellhounds, which were somehow being used in the mix - underneath the trailer - being used as "Guard Dogs". My friend, found them lurking around, when he called the Cable company. I never saw anyone run so quickly! That was one scared man. When you see a big, burly man, you do not expect to witness them running from the scene like a little girl!

At first, we thought maybe he saw a snake or a gnarly spider. Then we asked him about it when he got into his work van. "There's a dog with flames coming from this animal, and the eyes were like snake eyes. There were four of them with giant sharp teeth. You need an

Animal Control to come here before I ever go under their!"

This man was so scared, that his face was a pale white, as if he witnessed his first ghost. His heart was racing, and I strongly urged him to go see a doctor or the hospital. He was not looking so good.

My friend and I were tripping even more after finding that out, the sun was starting to set, and we had to figure something out. Shortly after, we went back inside, and gathered various weapons he had consumed over the past several months. We thought we would have to use them for protection. Then we encountered something stranger, the floors were moving like wave ripples on top of water. Then the floorboards were being pushed up -from underneath - as if it were a scene from *Harry & the Henderson's* movie.

We were not sure what to expect when nightfall came, and we could not call the Police with the illegal drugs & weapons out in the open. Therefore, we were on our own. It took until sunup the following day to resolve the major issue with those strange Hellhounds, but it was a long night to say the least.

My point to that story is it actually happened. It was not due to the drugs, as we thought. There was the cable man who confirmed it to be true.

Oh, and get this. There was an abandoned building behind my friend's trailer. It was a good football field away, but still within seeing the Federal agents taking pictures on the daily. After I stopped going after that long and incredible week, my friends trailer was raided be the Feds, and L.A. swat team. He was arrested for possession of narcotics, and the nearby neighbors were arrested for the drug manufacturing underneath the trailer. Apparently, an unknown agency - from the government - had shown up, just before my friend was hauled off to jail. He believed these trio of men were thereof, the M.I.B. as we have all learned to know them by.

About four months later, my friend was released from jail, and things were obviously different. We no longer used drugs, and we never spoke about that strange evening with the hellhounds.

Shortly before my friend was released from jail, I was diagnosed with a brain tumor. When he was released, he was not surprised any. Moreover, we both had a mutual feeling it was implanted by persons unknown. Every time I had to go in for an MRI, there were military intelligences in the building next door. It was all to ironic & quintessence for them to be next to every facility I had went to for my MRI scans, and doctors even.

When I had moved to New York, and eventually had went through the process again, they were no longer following me that closely.

I am guessing the things that went on at my friend's house, and the various events we had encountered during our drug phase, was no longer an imminent problem to these unknown agencies. Thankfully, of course!

Chapter 6

Moving ahead to the most recent incidents, would have to be 2010 and up. Keep in mind; this is still before my brain surgery removal of the brain tumor in 2012.

My wife and I had noticed the major activity of UFO's nearby our area in 2010. As far as we knew, we were not being abducted or anything like that. Nevertheless, we were seeing countless UFO's in the sky every week. Usually, it was like once or twice a year. There was a time, when she thought I was a bit nutty, because she was not seeing any of these things. Then she too, had started seeing these spaceships fly freely in our skies in upstate NY.

Moving on to 2012, I had my brain surgery in June, and I was satisfied with the results, I did not die on the table...and I was on the right road to recovery. I was in the middle of writing my first science fiction novel, and I was afraid of not being able to finish it with brain surgery. Boy was I wrong on that assumption. I not only finished it, but I also rewrote it!

My first book was finished, then edited in March of 2014, and then released April 17, and I have been continuing my career since.

The downfall on the recovery from

brain surgery, is I cannot hold down an
actual job, and I am forced to stay at
home, and do house chores, and grocery
shopping. I have not been on disability
as I obviously should be. Therefore, we
have been living off my wife's paychecks
through Retail, and it is not
substantial enough in pay. My wife is
unable to ever be promoted (as to the
fact is, they only promote the stupid
and brainwashed employees...which my
wife is neither). Her pay will never
increase, and she is constantly being
harassed by the managers on staff,
amongst the many regular associates. If
I had better connection {and was given
the opportunity by a publisher}, we

would not only be in this situation; but out of the rut, we have constantly been stuck in.

Aside from our current well-being, we have noticed many things in the past year. 2013 was a big year for the strangeness. We have both experienced time lapses while driving, and gaps in our memory. There was one time, we were at the movies, and we had both witnessed something incredibly strange. There was a laser beam coming from the middle of the screen, which projected to the audience, my wife & I were the only ones who thankfully had shut our eyes. I do not know why, but we had a mutual feeling of it about to happen. I peeked looking down to the people - not the

screen - and saw the laser going left to

right scanning everyone in the theater.

It was a strange event. After we had

left, no one was talking; it were as if

they are all drones and were not allowed

to talk. We proceeded to leave the

theater, and head home. Perhaps 5

minutes into the drive, and the road we

were on, I noticed a strangeness to the

"fog" in the road we were approaching.

Over two's of time was missing from

when we had approached the mysterious

fog. It was daytime when we had

approached the fog, and when we found

ourselves almost home, it was in the

evening, and I found myself driving, to

a different song entirely that was on the radio. We had both had this strange sensation of a head-rush, to a dizzy spell feeling. When we got home, we took a walk so our neighbor's would hear us talking. We were both very confused.

Nearing the end of 2013, I started to take pictures with my camera, and I started to become obsessed with taking pictures in our night's sky. I started getting pictures of the lights that illuminated off these awesome UFO's. Then not long after that, nothing had happened for months.

In the summer of 2014 (last year), I started witnessing UFO's nearby, with light shooting down from underneath the spacecraft. As if, it were sending or even retrieving something. It was magnificent, and yet scary. I was glad it was not that close to me, but it was close enough to see what can illuminate from the bottom.

Then in December of 2014, I had an abduction experience, and even released a short book about it. I vividly remember leaving my room after both my wife, and I had went to bed. It was around three in the morning when this happened to me. I was escorted to a ship by a robotic creature, which was a bit scary. I thought I was being abducted for the experimentation side of things. Luckily, I was not - to my knowledge - and I found myself inside the spaceship, in outer space. I remember seeing Earth, as of a picture taken from a Satellite.

I was overwhelmed at first; I was not sure the reasoning for me being inside the ship. Not to mention, these Alien beings were similar to humans. Only, they did not literally speak as we do. They speak telepathically. They spoke many languages, new & old, and many foreign. At first, I was confused about the language, because I never heard it before, and then not long into the talking, I started to understand it, and then I was speaking in this foreign tongue as well. The walls of the UFO

was layered with gold & diamonds. It
was magnificent.

I later came to found out that
these beings are quite similar to the
ones found in or nearby Venus & Agartha
(underground on Earth). I was there
with others, which were merely there for
a lesson. I also received warnings of
what could happen if the government or
their agencies decided to watch over me.
However, I am here for a purpose. Being
an amazing author of my generation is
one of them, and I plan to pursue it
with the doors wide open. If harm comes
to me, then you will all know why. I am
speaking my mind, sharing my thoughts &
experiences. I am not knocking on their

doors, and I hope that they do not knock on mine. I am not afraid to die, but it is how I die that worries me. As the latest saying goes, "It is what it is!"

Just remember, things that you may have thought you were aware of, there are much more to the story you may have been led to believe. Another thing about this mysterious & magical planet is there are various dimensions we are completely unknown to. This includes (from what I am aware of) & not limited to, Hell, heaven, & the physical dimension that we live on.

The bible & religion is a lie, and is only the tip of the iceberg. Just keep your eyes & even your mind open to the various acts and hidden realities

around you.

Chapter 7:

Straight to the Lesson

I am fully aware, that this is way easier, said than done. We do not necessarily have to rise up, and stand up against these manipulators, but a little self-control will do the trick.

These manipulators will never go away. Especially, if you live in the city, it is easier to block most of it all out...when living in the country. However, we all need & want things. I believe it be necessary to have to rely on *our* self-discipline - don't you?

However, you can slowly change your spending methods. You can change your thinking & listening process as well.

I used to get annoyed with people that were happy 24/7. I found it to be an annoyance. However, I am now trying to join the club!

To do this, you have to Love yourself, respect all humans for what we are and where we came from, and learn to change your negativity into positives! As you are thinking, *Geez is that all?*

I know it seems like a lot to ask, but if you were, and are, anything like me, change seems like a nightmare. Especially, when you feel like it seems to be too much work. It is easy to feel self-pity; it is also easy to feel negative. It is a struggle to stay happy with all of the ups & downs in our daily lives. Loving yourself is the first step. I highly recommend reading or watching *"The Secret"*. This was recommended to me in the past, and it helped shape my thinking...Just ignore the religious part of the lesson...ha...ha!

I have learned a great deal about attraction, and positive thinking.

In closing, I hope you enjoyed reading this book. You can see I have been a busy new writer in my first year. After this one, I will be at five or so, complete titles of various Genre's.

There are signs from the Universe

everywhere; you just have to look for them. Be sure to keep your eyes open, start thinking for yourself (unless it is illegal). Moreover, most of all, believe that we are all here for a reason - whether you have learned what it is or not - you will find your way, as I have. We are all connected, and the Universe will help you along the way.

Do not get swindled by mindless games due to manipulation, free yourself. Do not fall into the trap, do not be a slave to society, be yourself, and you will soon be on your way. It does not matter your age or gender, you will find your way along your journey in life to be the better you!

As far as Aliens, demonology, Cryptology, Hellish forces, various dimensions, UFO's, and many other unexplained happenings on Earth, try not to go to deep into the different topics, especially in countries that are trying to cover up the reality of the truth. You may find yourself being the victim of an assignation. Stray from the lies, but do not discuss it where *others* will be listening to you. Just watch your back! If you find yourself being paranoid, because you think your phones are being bugged, or even being followed, and nobody believes you do not second-guess yourself, because you are probably accurate.

Perhaps change your location to living in the countryside! It is easier not be watched from the "eye" in the sky. The reason I am attempting to make you aware of being on the internet while researching such topics, is due to the fact, that the government has agencies tracking us all. It is not something that is a rumor - it is true. They shut my computer off once from home a few years ago, and attempted to fine me, before accessing any programs again. I had to have a *hacker* fix my computer, just to use it again. Therefore, be careful what you may land on during your research!

References:

www.bibliotecapleyades.net/

www.google.com/

www.wikipedia.com

If you would like to follow me:

Twitter/@bobbyrsimonds &

www.facebook.com/bobbyrsimonds;

I will be creating stories for the world to read, until the day I perish.

Just remember, *nothing is, as it seems...*